~ POSTCARDS FROM T

THE VILLAGES OF MANCHESTER

Chris E. Makepeace

First published in 1989 as "The Lost Villages of Manchester" by
S.B. Publications

This fully revised edition is published by Sigma Leisure – an
imprint of Sigma Press, 1 South Oak Lane, Wilmslow, Cheshire
SK9 6AR, England.

British Library Cataloguing in Publication Data
A CIP record for this book is available from the British Library.

ISBN: 1-85058-671-3

Typesetting and Design by: Sigma Press, Wilmslow, Cheshire.

Cover photograph: Slade Lane, Longsight

Printed by: MFP Design and Print

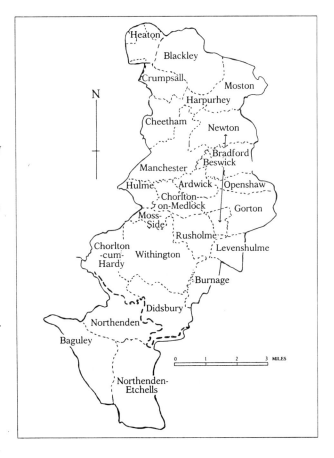

Preface

In the early twentieth century, the postcard – especially the picture postcard – was like the telephone today. They were extensively used to send messages to friends and relatives announcing a safe arrival at a destination, an intended visit or even sent as Christmas cards. As a result, picture postcards of virtually every town, suburb or village were published. In addition, people also appear to have had their own personal photographs turned into postcards and used these rather than purchase commercial ones.

The postcards reproduced in this volume cover the suburbs of Manchester rather than the city centre. Although there have been books on Manchester, this is the first time that all the suburbs have been covered in a single volume. This has posed problems in that the survival of postcards is not comprehensive. Some districts, especially those south of the city centre, and the suburbs where the more fortunate members of the community lived, are better covered than those to the north and east of Manchester or what are called today 'inner city' areas. However, virtually all the suburbs have been included and, wherever possible, I have illustrated these with postcards that have not been used before; in some cases, this has not been possible due to lack of suitable illustrations.

Many (but not all) of the areas covered in this volume were originally townships, centered on villages and hamlets and not part of Manchester. When the borough of Manchester was created in 1838, central Manchester was united with Hulme, Chorlton-on-Medlock, Ardwick and Cheetham to form the new local authority. It was not until 1885 that the first expansion of Manchester's boundaries took place when Rusholme and Bradford were included. Five years later, in 1890, most of what is now north and east Manchester (Blackley, Crumpsall, Moston, Openshaw and part of Gorton) joined Manchester. It was not until 1904 that many of the south districts, such as Moss Side, Withington, Didsbury and Chorlton-cum-Hardy, were taken over. In 1909, Levenshulme and the remainder of Gorton became part of Manchester and, finally, in 1931, Wythenshawe was split away from Cheshire to become part of Manchester. The result of the gradual mergers between Manchester and the surrounding areas was that Manchester developed into a long, thin city – as the map on the facing page shows.

The development of Manchester's suburbs was assisted by the gradual replacement of housing in the central area by offices, warehouses and shops and, also, by the growth of a public road transport system. The earliest public bus service ran in 1824, five years before London, a service which encouraged more and more businessmen to move away from the congested and unhealthy city centre. Places like Victoria Park, Greenheys and parts of Chorlton-on-Medlock were the first to benefit from this movement but with the development of the suburban railway network in the latter half of the nineteenth century, so areas further away from the city centre became ripe for development. The situation was gradually reached in the twentieth century that Manchester city centre became devoid of people living there and that most Mancunians lived in what were originally villages and hamlets surrounding a market town.

I hope that you, the reader, will find this an interesting book, especially as it has tried to cover all the suburbs rather than mixing central Manchester with its suburbs. If readers of this publication can fill any of the gaps which have been highlighted in the compilation of this volume – either in the form of postcards or information on some of the pictures – I shall be pleased to hear from them.

Chris E. Makepeace
5 Hilton Road
Disley
Cheshire SK12 2JU

Acknowledgements

I would like to take this opportunity to thank Sigma Press for reprinting this collection of illustrations showing Manchester suburbs, which formerly started out as villages or hamlets. I would also like to thank the staff of Manchester Local History Library (now the Local History Unit) for their help in the past and also David Brearley who copied some of the more faded illustrations for the book when it was first published. I must also express my grateful thanks to those who have saved postcards over the years or when they have found them hidden away, not thrown them out. Finally, my thanks are due to the support of my wife, Hilary, for checking the original manuscript and her constructive comments on the captions and choice of illustrations.

Contents

Tha Manchester Coat of Arms	1
Ardwick	2 - 4
Blackley	5 - 7
Bradford	8
Burnage	9
Cheetham	10 - 13
Chorlton-cum-Hardy	14 - 17
Chorlton-on-Medlock	18 - 32
Clayton	33 - 34
Collyhurst	35
Crumpsall	36 - 37
Didsbury	38 - 44
Fallowfield	45 - 46
Gorton	47 - 49
Harpurhey	50 - 51
Heaton Park	52 - 53

Hulme	*54 - 55*
Levenshulme	*56 - 61*
Longsight	*62 - 66*
Miles Platting	*67*
Moss Side	*68 - 71*
Moston	*72 - 74*
Newton Heath	*75*
Northenden	*76*
Openshaw	*77 - 78*
Rusholme	*79 - 83*
Trafford Park	*84 - 85*
Victoria Park	*86 - 89*
Whalley Range	*90 - 95*
Withington	*96 - 101*
Wythenshawe	*102 - 108*
Miscellaneous views	*109 - 112*

THE MANCHESTER COAT OF ARMS

This is the City's coat of arms after the opening of the Manchester Ship Canal in 1894, when the ship was added to it. One feature which has been on Manchester's arms since incorporation is the bee, a symbol of industry, which can be seen on the globe above the shield. The globe represents the world-wide trade of Manchester. Also incorporated in the arms are the arms of the Grelley family, who were the first Lords of the Manor of Manchester. The lion and the antelope, with the red rose, are drawn from the arms of Henry IV, Duke of Lancaster. The motto "Concilio et Labore" means "By council and hard work".

THE ARDWICK EMPIRE, 1906

The early 20th century saw the opening of many new theatres in Manchester. One was the Ardwick Empire, built by the Manchester Hippodrome and Ardwick Empire Ltd, whose managing director was Oswald Stoll. Designed by Fred Matcham, it seated about 3000 and was said to have had "good acoustics, ventilation, space and safety with an attractive decor". It opened on 18th July 1904 with seat prices from 3d to 2 shillings (10 pence in today's money). Before the First World War, there were two shows a night, often with well-known artists such as Fred Karno's Army. In 1935, when Stoll closed the Manchester Hippodrome on Oxford Street, he renamed the Ardwick Empire the "New Manchester Hippodrome" and had the interior remodelled. During the next 25 years, the theatre not only put on variety shows, but also musicals such as "The Student Prince". In 1961, the theatre was converted into a bowling alley. It was demolished in 1964 after being severely damaged in a fire.

STOCKPORT ROAD, ARDWICK, c. 1909
This view shows Stockport Road at its junction with Devonshire Street. The church on the right is Stockport Road Congregational Church, which was established in 1868 and moved into this building in 1889. The church, designed by F. W. Simon, was built of terracotta and brick and cost £5,370. On plan, it was an octagonal building with four long and four short sides. The church was closed in the 1960s and subsequently demolished.

POND ARDWICK GREEN

MANCHESTER

ARDWICK GREEN, ARDWICK, c. 1909

Ardwick Green was originally a private park for the benefit of the residents of Ardwick Green but, in 1867, it was acquired by Manchester Corporation and converted into a public park, which was much needed in the densely populated parts of Ardwick and the adjacent Chorlton-on-Medlock. The park covers three acres and, as the postcard shows, included a bandstand and two shallow pools, one of which is seen in the foreground.

Blackley, with Blackley Church, Manchester.

ST. PETER'S CHURCH, BLACKLEY

This postcard shows the centre of Blackley and its parish church, dedicated to St. Peter. The earliest reference to a religious establishment in the district is from 1360, when an oratory was licensed. Little is known about the chapel until 1549, after which references become more frequent. The chapel was rebuilt in 1736 and again in 1844. The Victorian church was built adjacent to the old chapel. Like other old established chapels which were to become parish churches in the nineteenth century, villages developed around them - as this card clearly shows.

(Postcard reproduced courtesy of Manchester Public Libraries)

ENTRANCE TO BOGGART HOLE CLOUGH.

ENTRANCE TO BOGGART HOLE CLOUGH, BLACKLEY, c. 1917

When Manchester acquired Boggart Hole Clough in 1894, the land was of poor quality and crossed by a deep valley, which made it unsuitable for agricultural or building use. When the land was acquired by the city, most of the vegetation was in poor condition but, over the years, the Parks Department has succeeded in improving the quality of the plant life and even introduced plants which will not grow anywhere else in the city. Another feature of the park is that it is never closed, as a public right of way runs through it - the entrance to which is shown here.

BOGGART HOLE CLOUGH, THE WAR MEMORIAL, BLACKLEY, c. 1924

The cessation of hostilities in November, 1918, left many communities wondering how to commemorate local people who had died in the war. In Blackley, £2,500 was raised to erect a memorial to the local people who had given their lives for their country. The site chosen was in a prominent location in Boggart Hole Clough, overlooking the district. The memorial consisted of "Victoria" with four smaller figures holding emblems of the army, navy, air force and nurses, and inscribed on it were the names of the dead. The unveiling, by Dr. H. Levinstein was attended by over 15,000 people, including the Lord Mayor and other civic leaders.

The Lake, Philips Park, Manchester.

PHILIPS PARK, BRADFORD, c. 1908

Philips Park was one of the first two parks to be opened in Manchester, in 1846. The cost of its purchase was raised by public subscription. It covered thirty acres and, as well as its ornamental flower beds and walks, there was also a lake which attracted wild birds. This lake, shown here, was later shallowed and converted to a pool where children could paddle and sail model boats. The park also contained glass-houses which were used for propagating plants, but these were moved to nurseries, established at Carrington by the Corporation in 1890.

EAST AVENUE, BURNAGE GARDEN VILLAGE (No. 2)

BURNAGE GARDEN VILLAGE, BURNAGE, c. 1930

In 1906, a meeting held in Manchester resulted in the formation of Manchester Tenants Limited, which planned to build a model village on the edge of Manchester to provide housing of a good standard for ordinary working people. At the time of its construction, it was the first Garden Village in Manchester and was built on what was described as the largest field in the area, covering twelve acres. Most of the houses built at Burnage were semi-detached with bathrooms, hot and cold running water and electricity. As this postcard of East Avenue shows, there was plenty of planting to give the area a rural feel.

CHEETHAM HILL VILLAGE, CHEETHAM, c. 1905

This postcard shows Cheetham Hill Road at its junction with Derby Street. This road, originally known as York Street, was one of the main routes from Manchester to Bury. In the nineteenth century, there were a number of fine buildings to be seen in the district, particularly along Cheetham Hill Road, where there was St. Chad's Church, the Great Synagogue, Cheetham Assembly Rooms, offices of the Prestwich Board of Guardians and the Spanish and Portuguese Synagogue. However, as this view shows, there were also properties on a more domestic scale, consisting mostly of shops with either living accommodation or workshops on the upper floors.

The Assize Courts, Manchester.

ASSIZE COURTS, CHEETHAM, c. 1904

The Assize Courts in Manchester were designed by Alfred Waterhouse prior to his winning the competition to design Manchester Town Hall. They were completed in 1864, at a cost of £100,000, and provided not only the court facilities, but also accommodation for judges attending the Assizes. The complex was completed in 1868 when Strangeways Prison, behind the Courts, was finished and opened.

Manchester Assize Courts, Crown Court.

INTERIOR OF CROWN COURT, ASSIZE COURTS, CHEETHAM

Although there are many illustrations of the exterior of the Assize Courts, ones showing the interior - as it was - are not so common. This postcard shows the interior of one of the courts which appears to have been designed to overawe both the accused and the witness. An interesting architectural detail was the use of various types of old forms of punishment to decorate the capitals of the columns in the entrance hall of the Courts.

CHEETHAM ASSIZE COURTS AFTER THE BLITZ, 1941

The 1940 Christmas blitz on Manchester resulted in only slight damage being sustained to the Assize Courts. However, on the night of 1st/2nd June, 1941 (Whit Sunday), there was a ninety-minute raid on the city. This raid, said to have been the most severe after the Christmas blitz, severely damaged a number of buildings including the Assize Courts. Other buildings damaged during the raid included the Woolpack public house, opened in 1864; and a favourite hostelry with members of the legal profession attending the courts.

CHANDOS ROAD, CHORLTON-CUM-HARDY, c. 1924

During the latter years of the nineteenth century, Chorlton began to expand, encouraged by the arrival of the railway in 1881 and, later, by improvements to Wilbraham Road. Several new streets were erected off Wilbraham Road, with large semi-detached houses - like the ones shown in this picture of Chandos Road. These houses were built towards the end of the first decade of the twentieth century and were within easy walking distance of the railway station; they were given names like "Norwood", "Ash Hurst" and "Shrubbery Bank".

RECREATION GROUNDS, CHORLTON-CUM-HARDY, c. 1904

Chorlton Recreation Ground was given to Chorlton by Lord Egerton and was opened on 16th May, 1896. It was laid out on what had formerly been known as Half Acre Field, on Beech Lane, and was Chorlton's only public park until Chorlton Park was made in 1928. The facilities that were provided for children were limited - if this postcard is any guide - there being only see-saws. The writer of this card, sent in 1904, claims to spend four hours a day here! One wonders whether she was a nanny and this was where she brought the children in her care, during the day.

BARLOW MOOR ROAD, CHORLTON-CUM-HARDY, c. 1912

Barlow Moor Road is one of the main roads through Chorlton, linking Old Trafford with Didsbury. It probably started as a track, but as Chorlton began to grow, it assumed the appearance of a suburban street with houses, churches and shops. This postcard, although posted in 1927, dates from several years earlier as the chemist's shop at the end of the arcade was a draper's shop in 1927. In that year, the other shops occupying the arcade included a draper, milliner, shoemaker (Timpson's), tobacconist, confectioner and wine and spirit merchant.

THE MANCHESTER CREMATORIUM, BARLOW MOOR ROAD, from the Air

THE MANCHESTER CREMATORIUM, BARLOW MOOR ROAD, CHORTLON-CUM-HARDY

In the 1880s, the crematorium movement gained increasing support. A society was formed in Manchester, in 1887, to increase public awarenesss of the benefits of cremation which lead, in 1890, to the formation of the Manchester Crematorium Company. Land was acquired in Chorlton-cum-Hardy and, in 1892, the Crematorium was opened. It was designed by Steinthall and Salomons and was the first complete crematorium to be erected in this country. (The first crematorium as such to be opened was at Guildford, a few years earlier). The aerial view was taken in the inter-war years and shows not only the rural setting of the Crematorium, but also new housing off Mauldeth Road West.

(Photograph reproduced courtesy the Board of Manchester Crematorium Co. Ltd.)

OXFORD STREET AND THE REFUGE ASSURANCE CO OFFICES. MANCHESTER

OXFORD ROAD, CHORLTON-ON-MEDLOCK, c. 1920

The railway bridge, carrying the line between London Road (now Piccadilly) Station and Oxford Road Station, marks the point where Oxford Street becomes Oxford Road and, also, where Chorlton-on-Medlock begins. Oxford Street was started in 1792 and, at this point, was built on an embankment above the flood plain of the River Medlock. The material from the embankment was excavated from a near-by area which later became notorious as Little Ireland. All the other buildings in the foreground, which are in Chorlton-on-Medlock, were demolished during the 1920s and 1930s whilst those in the background can still be seen today.

ALL SAINTS, OXFORD ROAD, CHORLTON-ON-MEDLOCK, c. 1904

This row of shops - 107 to 137 Oxford Road - was erected in the early 1820s as a terrace of houses called Grosvenor Place. For a short time, some of the properties were used solely for residential purposes and then, as the 1834 directory indicates, several became shops, with living accommodation on the upper floors. Around the time that this postcard was published, the shops were occupied by a music seller, hosier, boot maker, house furnisher, furrier, milliner, mantle maker, photographer, hair dresser, bookseller, tea dealer (Burgons, who were there for almost a century), a post office and the Union Bank of Manchester (now Barclays Bank).

19

'ALL SAINTS' DEVONSHIRE ST MANCHESTER 25858.

ALL SAINTS CHURCH, CHORLTON-ON-MEDLOCK, c. 1905

The demolition of All Saints Church in 1949, after serious damage during the blitz, removed one of Manchester's landmarks. The church, consecrated in 1820, was Grecian in style and octagonal in plan, but the erection of the tower in 1835 altered its appearance. Surrounding the churchyard was an extensive graveyard in which over 16,500 people were buried between 1820 and its closure in 1881. In 1906, the graveyard was taken over by Manchester City Council and was landscaped. On the Lower Ormond Street side of the churchyard, a children's playground was constructed, a facility which was much needed in an area where land for parks and playgrounds was in short supply.

CAVENDISH CONGREGATIONAL CHURCH, STRETFORD ROAD, CHORLTON-ON-MEDLOCK, c. 1906

Cavendish Congregational Church opened in 1848 as a replacement for Mosley Street Congregational Chapel and was designed by Edward Walters in the Early English Style. It cost £30,000 and was dominated by a 171ft. spire. The church was closed in 1969 and demolished four years later. The postcard also shows Paulden's shop, on the right. Paulden's was established in 1865 and moved to these premises in 1879. William Paulden's philosophy was to have a large turnover with small profits which kept prices down and attracted large numbers of customers. Pauldens was one of the earliest shops in Manchester to be lit by electric lighting. In 1957, a serious fire destroyed the building but the store continued, moving to vacant premises on Market Street.

CONGREGATIONAL CHURCH CAVENDISH St MANCHESTER

Owens College, Manchester. 341.

OWEN'S COLLEGE, OXFORD ROAD, CHORLTON-ON-MEDLOCK, c. 1906

Owen's College (now Manchester University) was founded in 1851 and moved to its present site on Oxford Road in 1873. The original buildings around the quadrangle were designed by Alfred Waterhouse, whose son was involved in the design of some of the later buildings, including Whitworth Hall, completed in 1903. This card gives an unusual view of the University showing as it does the Burlington Street facade of the buildings, including the block housing the Christie Library.

Christy's Library, Victoria University Manchester

**MANCHESTER UNIVERSITY CHRISTIE LIBRARY, OXFORD ROAD
CHORLTON-ON-MEDLOCK, c. 1908**

When Owen's College moved to its Oxford Road site, a library was planned but nothing had been built by 1892, when the College was presented with the library of the late Professor Freeman. Richard Copley Christie, a former professor and, later one of the governors of the College, offered to build a library at his own expense. His generous offer was accepted and the new library, designed by Alfred Waterhouse and named after the donor, was completed in 1895. It was formally opened in 1898. This view shows the first floor which consisted of a room 124ft. long by 40ft. wide by 20ft. high that was used as a reading room and a reference library.

**MANCHESTER UNIVERSITY DANCE, OXFORD ROAD, CHORLTON-ON-MEDLOCK
FEBRUARY 1920**

Although captioned "Manchester University Dance - Feb 16. 1920", this postcard shows some of the students who attended the dance which took place after the Rag Day Procession on Shrove Tuesday 1920. Some of those attending are in their usual dress but the majority of the students at this annual event - later known as Rag Ball - are in fancy dress.

Church of Holy Name, Manchester.

HOLY NAME CHURCH, OXFORD ROAD, CHORLTON-ON-MEDLOCK, c. 1912

Holy Name Church was designed by Hanson & Son of London and is in the Gothic style of the thirteenth century. The church replaced a temporary church opened in 1868. The new church was opened in 1871 by the Marquis of Ripon. It will be noticed that there is no octagonal top to the tower - a feature which makes the church such a landmark today. This was designed by A. G. Scott and added in 1928, in memory of Father Bernard Vaughan who was at the church from 1888 to 1902. Today, the church is closed and there is a question-mark hanging over the future of this magnificent building.

Oxford Road, Manchester, from Nelson Street.

OXFORD ROAD, CHORLTON-ON-MEDLOCK, 1926

This view of Oxford Road will be familiar to many generations of students at Manchester University as it shows Oxford Road looking southwards towards the Royal Eye Hospital and the twin towers of Manchester Royal Infirmary. In the background is the tower of the Union Baptist Chapel, which stood on the corner of High Street, now Hathersage Road, and Oxford Road/Wilmslow Road. On the extreme left of the picture can be seen a small portion of a block of property erected in the early 20th century which was occupied around 1903 by dentists, doctors and private tutors.

ROYAL EYE HOSPITAL, OXFORD ROAD, CHORLTON-ON-MEDLOCK, c. 1914

The Royal Eye Hospital was founded in 1814 when W. J. Wilson, a well-known oculist, wrote to William Fox suggesting that a charity be established to provide relief for those poor who were afflicted with eye diseases. Its first premises were at the top of King Street. Over the next seventy years, the Hospital had several premises before moving, in 1886, to a new building on the corner of Nelson Street and Oxford Road. The new hospital was designed by Pennington and Bridgen and cost £25,000, including land and fittings. The cost was raised from many sources including local authorities in the region, trade unions, co-operative societies and private benefactors.

Victoria Hospital, Manchester.

MANCHESTER ROYAL INFIRMARY, OXFORD ROAD, CHORLTON-ON-MEDLOCK, c. 1920
This postcard is wrongly captioned "Victoria Hospital, Manchester". In fact, it is the main entrance to the Manchester Royal Infirmary on Oxford Road. The Infirmary moved to this site at the end of 1908 and was officially opened by Edward VII in July 1909. The new building more than doubled the number of beds available when compared with the old Infirmary building in Piccadilly. In addition, it was possible to make provision for new developments, such as the provision of special X-ray facilities, which had been in temporary and very unsuitable accommodation in the old building.

The Royal Infirmary Manchester

ST. MARY'S HOSPITAL, OXFORD ROAD, CHORLTON-ON-MEDLOCK, c. 1910
Although this illustration is entitled "The Royal Infirmary, Manchester", the main building in the foreground is that of St. Mary's Hospital. It was founded in 1790 to deal with women with gynaecological problems, maternity cases and children. After occupying several sites in Manchester and Salford, St. Mary's merged with the Southern Hospital for Women and Children. The merger of the two hospitals had been suggested as early as 1894, but agreement could not be reached. It was another ten years before the two organisations re-opened discussions on a merger. This time they were successful and a new hospital was built on High Street and opened in 1911.

WHITWORTH PARK

WHITWORTH ART GALLERY, OXFORD ROAD, CHORLTON-ON-MEDLOCK, c. 1911
Manchester is fortunate in that, as well as the City's Art Gallery on Mosley Street, there is another
fine collection of paintings housed at the Whitworth Art Gallery. This Gallery was originally administered
by a trust established on the death of Sir Joseph Whitworth. It was intended to provide facilities
for the display of collections of the fine arts as well as provide facilities for their research and study.
In 1958, the Gallery was given to Manchester University to secure its future and ensure its continuing
development. This postcard shows the side of the Gallery rather than the more usual front view.

THE LAKE, WHITWORTH PARK, MANCHESTER

WHITWORTH PARK, OXFORD ROAD, CHORLTON-ON-MEDLOCK, c. 1923

In 1904, Manchester leased eighteen acres of land from the Whitworth Trustees in order to create a children's park in Chorlton-on-Medlock. No adult facilities were provided except for a bandstand to entertain parents and others who were looking after children. In the centre of the park was a lake which, in the 1920s, was shallowed to enable children to paddle and sail their model boats on it. This postcard shows a group of children at the lake - with a fishing-net and jam-jars; they had presumably been looking for pond-life. One wonders whether this was in connection with school or just childhood curiosity as to what one can find in lakes and ponds.

31

BILTON'S MARIONETTES, HYDE GROVE, CHORLTON-ON-MEDLOCK

This is a good example of a postcard that was used for advertising purposes. In the directories, Percy Bilton was described as a "musician" and is recorded as living at Hyde Grove between 1927 and 1969. The Marionettes were probably part of an entertainment provided by Mr. Bilton at parties such as those organised by schools and Sunday schools. Presumably, Mr. Bilton is the gentleman standing on the right of the card, whilst his audience appear to be seated in a hall and the marionettes are on the stage.

CLAYTON HALL, CLAYTON, c. 1914

Clayton Hall is the last of the halls within Manchester's boundaries to retain its moat. The Hall stands on the site of an earlier building and it is probably for that building that the moat was created. The present Hall dates from the sixteenth century and has undergone several alterations over the years. There was a major restoration of the building by Alfred Darbishire for Manchester City Council, when they acquired it in 1893. This postcard clearly shows not only the Hall, but also the bridge which crosses the moat to provide access to the building. The Hall's most famous resident was Humphrey Chetham who died in 1653 and left money to found a school - Chetham's School - and a free public library - Chetham's Library.

Clayton Sports. 1914.

CLAYTON SPORTS, CLAYTON, 1914

This postcard shows a cycle race at Clayton Sports in 1914. It is interesting to note that the riders are dressed in the costumes of various countries of the British Empire. Although it has not been possible to trace the exact date of the event, the fact that the contestants are in these costumes leads one to wonder whether it took place on Empire Day that year.

CHANCEL, ALBERT MEMORIAL CHURCH.

ALBERT MEMORIAL CHURCH, COLLYHURST, c. 1910

Albert Memorial Church, completed in 1864, was dedicated to the memory of the Prince Consort. The building was designed by John Lowe and cost £2,400, the money being raised through a public appeal. Throughout its history, the Albert Memorial Church was renowned for its evangelical bible preaching, including Saturday evening prayer and praise meetings and mid-week bible readings. The interior of the church, shown here and described as "gaunt, barn-like, with an open timber roof", could seat almost 700 people. In 1972, the church was closed and demolished as part of a rationalisation of the Anglican churches in the Collyhurst area.

OLD COTTAGES. CRUMPSALL GREEN.

CRUMPSALL GREEN, CRUMPSALL, c. 1903

Crumpsall Green was a small area on Crumpsall Road and was probably the centre of the original settlement in the area. These cottages give the impression of dating back to at least the eighteenth century, but their rendered exteriors may hide evidence of their earlier construction. In 1903, the directory records four households as living at Crumpsall Green: Frederick William Stretton at Willow House; Edward S. Partington, a farmer at Ivy House; William Henry Grindrod, traveller and John Dixon, a grocer. It is probable that one of these two latter people lived in the cottages shown on this postcard.

C.W.S. CRUMPSALL PHYSICAL CULTURE EXERCISE.
No. 2   DUMB BELLS.

C.W.S. WORKS, CRUMPSALL

The C.W.S. moved into the field of producing goods for sale about 1873, when it opened a factory in Crumpsall for the manufacture of "biscuits, sweets and currant bread etc.". This factory gradually grew in size and was the first of the C.W.S. factories to provide a sports ground for those employed there. These facilities were augmented after World War I by facilities for indoor recreation and physical exercise. This postcard shows a group of employees from the Crumpsall Works undertaking what is described as "physical culture", in a part of the factory which has been set aside for recreational purposes.

ST. JAMES'S CHURCH, DIDSBURY, c. 1910

St. James's was established in 1235 and became a parochial chapel in 1352 when a graveyard was created for the benefit of plague victims. It was built in an elevated position overlooking the River Mersey and must have been a landmark for travellers crossing the river. In 1620, the church was rebuilt and the tower added. Further alterations were made in the eighteenth century but, in the nineteenth century, the church was almost completely rebuilt, with the exception of the tower. Today, the church is not in the centre of the village, as it was in earlier times, but set in a quiet area, just off the busy Wilmslow Road.

DIDSBURY LIBRARY AND WAR MEMORIAL

DIDSBURY LIBRARY, WILMSLOW ROAD, DIDSBURY, c. 1925
Didsbury Library was opened in 1911, on the site of the bowling green which had belonged to the Grey Mare public house. It was paid for by Andrew Carnegie and is typical in design of many of the Carnegie Libraries. Although the building was paid for by Carnegie, the books had to be provided by the local authority. The spire in the background is that of Emmanuel Church on Barlow Moor Road which was opened in 1858. On the right is Didsbury's memorial to those residents who gave their lives during World War I.

WILMSLOW ROAD, DIDSBURY, c. 1904

This is how the centre of Didsbury looked around 1904. It shows Wilmslow Road looking north towards Withington, from its junction with Hardman Street (now School Lane) and Barlow Moor Road. The low wall in the centre surrounds the coal yard of the Bridgewater Colliery Company, which had been in Didsbury since 1858. The gabled buildings beyond were erected in 1881, whilst the site of the shops on the extreme right was redeveloped sometime between 1904 and 1914. When the card was issued, these three shops were occupied by, from left to right: Charles Owen, draper; Joseph Jones, fruiterer and John Ashworth, draper.

ELM ROAD, DIDSBURY, c. 1909

Elm Road came into existence in the early twentieth century when Parkfield House was demolished and its drive, leading to Barlow Moor Road, was widened and the land sold for development. The houses, which were erected along this tree-lined road, were three-storeyed and many exhibit an architectural feature of the period; namely the use of "black and white" boarding at the upper levels to give the buildings a more "English" appearance. When this card was posted, there were only 16 houses on Elm Road, all of which were named. Elm Road was ideally situated for Manchester businessmen, being close to the Midland Railway Station at West Didsbury and the terminus of the electric tram at the junction of Barlow Moor Road and Palatine Road.

West Didsbury.

Red Bank Farm and River Mersey.

RIVER MERSEY, DIDSBURY, c. 1908

The River Mersey is the traditional boundary between Lancashire and Cheshire. (The name Mersey actually means "boundary water".) This postcard shows the Mersey in West Didsbury with Red Bank Farm in the background. The farm itself was in two separate townships; the fields being in Didsbury and the farmhouse in Chorlton-cum-Hardy. It is unclear whether the fields named "Great Red Bank" and "Little Red Bank" on the mid-nineteenth century Tithe Map were part of the farm, but, if so, they were being farmed by John Rudd. The name of the farm and the field may be derived from the existence of a sandstone outcrop, which was not an unusual way to name a place or fields in earlier centuries.

DIDSBURY SHOW, 1910

The first modern agricultural show in Didsbury took place in 1901, but, as France and Woodall point out, there were advertisements for agricultural shows in the area in the early nineteenth century. The Didsbury show was organised by a society known as the South Manchester Show and the event was held on land owned by Lord Simon of Wythenshawe, free of charge, on the first Monday in August. This postcard shows the judging of one of the events: namely for horse and carriage. In the background can be seen some of the large crowd which attended the event in 1910. The Didsbury Show ceased after 1966 when Manchester took over the fields and refused to allow them to be used for the Show on August Mondays.

43

PALATINE ROAD, DIDSBURY, c. 1903

In 1901, electric trams were introduced into Manchester. Gradually, horse-buses and horse-trams operated by the Manchester Carriage and Tramways Company, were phased out. On some routes, however, it was regarded as uneconomic to lay tracks and erect overhead wires so horse-buses continued to operate until the arrival of the motor-bus. One such route was from Cheadle, which continued to operate until 1906. These horse-buses did not go into Manchester, but terminated at the junction of Barlow Moor Road and Palatine Road, where the electric tramways ended. This postcard shows the Cheadle horse-bus as it approaches the end of its journey along Palatine Road, Didsbury.

THE BOULEVARDS, FALLOWFIELD, c. 1914

Although this postcard is entitled the "Boulevards, Fallowfield", the view is actually of Wilmslow Road, looking towards Manchester. On the left, there is one of the entrances to Platt Fields, which was originally the entrance to a large house called "Ashfield" which had been purchased by Manchester in 1913, demolished and the grounds added to Platt fields. Hidden behind the trees is Platt Chapel, which dates back to the late seventeenth century. On the right is the wall of the "Oaks", which was owned by the Behrens family until they passed it to Manchester University to become a hall of residence.

45

FALLOWFIELD STATION, 1909

Fallowfield Station was opened in October 1891 when the first section of the Manchester, Sheffield and Lincolnshire Railway's line between Chorlton Juntion and Fairfield was completed. The station cost £13,025 and was built by J. D. Nowell. It never had a frequent service as the trams provided a quicker and more direct route into Manchester. The line itself was not finished until the following year. When it was completed, it provided the company with a direct link between Central Station and its line to Sheffield from London Road Station.

CROSS LANE, GORTON

Until 1890, Gorton was an independent local board of health outside Manchester. Consequently, it attracted a lot of industry which, in its turn, attracted people to come and live in the area. Between 1851 and 1901, Gorton's population rose from 4,476 to 55,417. To serve the people, shops developed like those shown at the junction of Cross Street and Wellington Road. Virtually every type of small shop was to be found on Cross Lane ranging from butchers and grocers to hairdressers and drapers. Amongst the more unusual ones at this time was an emigration agent and several fried-fish dealers. The house on the right of the picture looks as if it might have been a former toll-house, by its shape and the blocked window facing the road.

(Picture reproduced courtesy Manchester Public Libraries)

DEBDALE PARK, GORTON, 1930
In 1912, Manchester Corporation Waterworks Department decided that they had land in Gorton which they did not want and so it was taken over by the Parks Department and laid out as a park. Much of the land was devoted to sporting activities, there being tennis courts, bowling greens, 8 football pitches and cricket pitches. Despite the proximity of a large area of water, no water sports facilities were allowed by the Waterworks Department. The building on the left of the picture was erected between 1926 and 1927 for the benefit of those playing tennis and bowls.

CORONATION CELEBRATIONS, GORTON, 1937

The Coronation of H.M. King George VI was celebrated by official functions organised by the City Council, which included a civic service and treats for children and old people. The Lord Mayor expressed a wish that all parts of the city celebrated the Coronation, even the poorer quarters. Street committees organised events for residents including tea parties for children. This postcard shows the residents of a Gorton street, presumably during a street party.

WHIT WALK, HARPURHEY

Whit Walks were not and are not confined to the spectacular ones which take place in the centre of Manchester. Many of the suburban churches organise walks around the parish ending up either in a public park or at the parish church. The walks were not restricted to one particular religious denomination. This particular procession was of Harpurhey Wesleyan Methodists in Queen's Park.

Although it is undated, the costume of those taking part suggests that it may be from the early 1920s.

QUEEN'S PARK, HARPURHEY, c. 1904

Queen's Park was one of the first two public parks to be opened in Manchester. It covered 29 acres overlooking the valley of the River Irk. The land on which it was laid contained only a small area suitable for use for games so that during the 1920s and 1930s, Manchester used unemployed men to level parts of it so that tennis courts could be constructed. The house in the background of this card was transformed from a gentlemen's residence into Queen's Park Art Gallery and Museum (such facilities being regarded as important adjuncts to public parks in the mid-19th century). The statue of Ben Brierley, the well-known 19th-century dialect writer and poet, was erected by public subscription in 1888.

Heaton Hall, Heaton Park.

HEATON HALL, c. 1907

Heaton Hall was the home of the Earls of Wilton until it was sold in 1902 to meet death duties.
The hall was designed by James Wyatt and replaced an earlier timber-framed building. When the
hall and the estate were sold, Manchester City Council purchased it for £230,000 to prevent it being
sold for either residential or industrial development as Trafford Park had been. The purchase of
Heaton Park gave Manchester its largest park and an open space, the value of which far exceeded
its cost of purchase.

BOATING LAKE, HEATON PARK

When Heaton Park was acquired by Manchester, the Corporation did not attempt to landscape it like other parks, but decided to leave it as parkland and there was even a suggestion that herds of deer might be introduced as an added attraction. However, there were certain features added such as the boating lake shown here. This lake also became a haven for wild life, as well as a popular resort for visitors to the park. The park also became one of the regular venues for Whit week outings by Sunday schools from inner city Manchester as access was easy by tram car.

GREAT JACKSON STREET, HULME, c. 1908

Great Jackson Street was originally a country lane, but as Hulme developed in the nineteenth century, it became one of the most important roads in the district, passing through the heart of the area and linking Stretford Road with Chester Road. Great Jackson Street was essentially a street of small shop-keepers and businesses although intersperced between the shops were private houses, identified in the directory as householders. This view appears to have been taken looking from Chester Road towards Stretford Road, close to where City Road intersected it. The public house may be the Tramway Public House on the corner of Leinster Street.

(Postcard reproduced courtesy Manchester Public Libraries)

WHITE CITY, HULME c. 1907

In 1827, the Botanical and Horticultural Society was founded in Manchester with the expressed aim to encourage the study of botany and horticulture. Sixteen acres of ground were laid out on the edge of Manchester and planted with trees and shrubs and later, more exotic plants were added when a splendid glass house was erected. Towards the end of the 19th century, interest declined and early in the 20th century, the site was sold to Heathcote and Brown, who opened an amusement park about 1905. This, they named, White City Pleasure Grounds. Amongst the attractions were a waterchute, a big dipper and hot air balloon, which presumably took visitors up for a view of Manchester from the air. In the background can be seen the chimneys of the factories in Trafford Park, which so radically changed the appearance of the area at the end of the 19th century.

LEVENSHULME c. 1907

Levenshulme enjoyed a separate existence from Manchester until an overwhelming majority of its electorate voted to join its largest neighbour in 1909. This postcard shows four of the district's main buildings: St. Peter's Church, established in 1852; the Library, opened in 1902; the Wesleyan Mission Church; the local school; and the bowling green, possibly in Cringle Fields.

Levenshulme Tram Terminus.

Well! How are you. You are too long time for write to me. M. L.

STOCKPORT ROAD, LEVENSHULME, c. 1906

This view of Levenshulme in the early 20th century shows the centre of the district, where **Albert Road, Stockport Road** and **Cromwell Grove** meet. Clearly visible on the right is the **Railway Inn**, which looks as if it was built in the 1840s and may have started as a beer house. Almost **opposite it was the Pack Horse Hotel**, which claims to have been licensed in the 16th century and which proudly proclaims to have been rebuilt in 1907. The tall block of buildings on the right is called "**New Market Place**" and was built in the 1890s, at a time when there were many new properties being built in Levenshulme.

ALBERT ROAD, LEVENSHULME, c. 1905

This Edwardian postcard shows Albert Road, one of the main roads into Levenshulme. The most obvious feature is the railway bridge and entrance to Levenshulme Station. The station, on the main line between Manchester and Stockport, was opened in 1842. With the opening of the station, the journey time into Manchester was reduced to less than 10 minutes which resulted in the rise in popularity of Levenshulme as a residential suburb for the more fortunate members of Manchester society.

Burnage Lane, Levenshulme.

The Bee Series.

BURNAGE LANE, LEVENSHULME, 1903

In the 19th century, Burnage Lane and Slade Lane joined near Cringle Brook. Most of the road lay in Burnage, but the section illustrated here must have been the small portion which lay within the boundaries of Levenshulme. It is probable that the cottage on the right is **Cringle Brook Cottage** whilst the large house on the left was Northbrook House, which later became the nurses home to the Duke of York Hospital.

126c   DELAMERE ROAD (FROM ESSEX STREET) LEVENSHULME, M/C   J.L.B. Bann...

DELAMERE ROAD, LEVENSHULME, c. 1910

Delamere Road was built in the early 20th century at a time when there was much new building in the district. The houses built at this time were erected to much higher standards than others in other areas around Manchester, standards which took the rest of Manchester almost 20 years to reach after Levenshulme had been amalgamated with Manchester in 1909.

UNEMPLOYED CAMP, LEVENSHULME, 1908
Around 1908, the Manchester area suffered a period of high unemployment. In order to alleviate distress and hardship, public works were initiated, such as the laying out of **Platt Fields Park**. Other ideas which were tried at the time included the establishment of a camp for the unemployed in Levenshulme, as shown in this postcard. The camps were run on **military lines and the aim appears** to have been to give those unemployed something to do rather than **hang around street corners**.

LONGSIGHT, c. 1906

Longsight became part of Manchester in 1885 by which time it was beginning to expand rapidly, as increasing numbers of people were forced to move away from central Manchester due to the increasing number of commercial buildings there. Despite the existence of streets of terraced houses, Longsight also had several interesting buildings which are shown here. Worthy of mention is Slade Hall (top right), which dates back to the 16th century and can still be seen today. The entrance to Belle Vue, the Wesleyan Chapel and Ivy Chapel have now been demolished; the card providing a record of them for posterity.

Birch Lane, Longsight.

BIRCH LANE, LONGSIGHT, 1909

Birch is a common element of many streets on the boundaries of Longsight and Levenshulme. The name is taken from the Birch family who were extensive landowners in the area in the 17th and 18th centuries. Many of the houses on Birch Lane were built in the last half of the 19th century and were intended for professional people and small businessmen. The proximity to Victoria Park as well as a good tram service into Manchester encouraged these people to move out to what was a very pleasant area to live at the beginning of the 20th century.

Kirkmanshulme Lane, Longsight.

KIRKSMANSHULME LANE, LONGSIGHT, c. 1909

Kirksmanshulme Lane links Stockport Road with Hyde Road and for most of its western side, it follows the perimeter of Belle Vue. This view, looking from Stockport Road, shows the railway bridge carrying the main line to London in the background together with some of the houses built towards the end of the 19th century. It is interesting that these houses all have small front gardens with what appears to be the obligatory tree to provide colour and shade. The type of person living here in the early 20th century included commercial travellers, engineers, warehousemen and small manufacturers.

ZOOLOGICAL GARDENS.
BELLE VUE, MANCHESTER.

BELLE VUE

Belle Vue was started by John Jennison as pleasure grounds in 1829 in **Adswood** (Stockport). In 1836, Jennison acquired the site of Belle Vue House, Hyde Road where there was room for expansion. As well as exotic animals, Belle Vue was famous for its amusement facilities which included a maze, a large artificial lake and a large dancing floor, shown here. In the background of the postcard can be seen the set constructed for the fireworks displays for which Belle Vue was renowned. The sets represented events either from history, such as the Lisbon Earthquake, or current events like the Afghan Wars.

LNWR FLOWER SHOW, BELLE VUE, LONGSIGHT, 1912

On 17th August 1912, the fifth annual flower show of the London, North Western Railway Company (North Eastern Division) was held at Belle Vue. Two cups were competed for: the Founder's Cup for those from the Manchester and district division and the Yorkshire Cup for the Yorkshire division. Among the awards were ones for the best railway station gardening, and flowers grown in signal-box window-boxes.

OLDHAM ROAD, MILES PLATTING, 1906

Miles Plating is divided by Oldham Road. Although there is industry in the area, this postcard shows some of the cottages which could be seen in the early 20th century on Oldham Road. These cottages appear to be of the "two-up and two-down" variety with small front gardens, indicating that they were intended to be rented by those skilled working people who could afford to pay slightly higher rents for a better type of house. Amongst the group on the picture are two boys named John and Willie. We know they are there because Lizzie sent the card and asked the recipient, Miss A. Taylor of Rochdale, if she could identify them.

ALEXANDRA ROAD, MOSS SIDE, 1906

This view shows the east side of Alexandra Road looking towards Manchester from its junction with **Bold Street**. The tower is that of St. Mary' Church, Upper Moss Lane, designed by J. S. Crowther and built between 1856 and 1858. In 1906, the shops on this section of road included Salter & Salter (1900) Ltd. **(bootmakers), Fecht & Sons (drapers)**, M. & A. Scott (umbrella makers), H. E. Gorton (beer retailers), W. Irving (confectioner), **Pendleton's** (provision merchants), Maypole Dairy Co. (butter factors), Mrs. H. Ribbons (eating house), G. Southern (butcher), Mrs. A. Kershaw (stationer), J. Jackson (tailor), W. Timpson (bootmaker), Mrs. J. Moore (draper and hosier), Mrs. A. Wallworth (milliner), Truswell & Co. (boot and shoe manufacturers) and Shaw & **Magill** (jewellers).

MOSS SIDE HARRIERS, MOSS SIDE

Athletics was an important sport in late Victorian and Edwardian Manchester with many athletics meetings taking place. This postcard shows Moss Side Harriers and their officials outside their headquarters, which appears to be a public house. It is a pity that the name of the pub cannot be identified. It does, however, show that even in areas where conditions were not all that were to be desired, there were groups of men who were keen to participate in sporting activities and presumably bring honour to the area where they lived.

LLOYD STREET, MOSS SIDE, c. 1920
A well-known building on Lloyd Street was the Denmark Hotel. When it was built, this part of Moss Side was still a sought-after residential area with its large terraced houses, one of which can be seen on the right of the card. Despite the clearance of property in the area, some of the mid-19th century buildings still remain, but the Denmark Hotel does not. In the background is the roof of Christ Church, Moss Side, which was designed by Cecil Hardisty and built between 1899 and 1904.

Princess Road Higher Grade School, Moss Side.   *The Central Hall.*

PRINCESS ROAD BOARD SCHOOL, MOSS SIDE, 1903

Until 1904, Moss Side was an independent urban district council which had its own school board composed of representatives of various religious denominations rather than of various political parties. Princess Road School was built in 1895 to provide 600 places for local children in modern educational facilities. On the day it opened, over 800 children were enrolled. Within a short period, there were over 1000 pupils attending the school. In the early 20th century, a feature of the school was the fact that the walls were adorned with paintings and etchings whilst in the hall, shown here, there were tropical plants.

71

HOUGH HALL, MOSTON

Hough Hall, Moston is said to have been built for Hugh Shacklock, a merchant in the early 16th century. Later it became the property of the Halgh family, who owned it until the late 17th century, when it was sold again. Since that time, it has changed ownership many times. The hall was described in the mid-19th century as a picturesque timber-framed house with an ashlar basement on which there was "strong timber frame-work" infilled with brick. Although the hall still exists today, it is surrounded by buildings of Victorian and later origins.

Campo Santa, Moston Cemetery

ST. JOSEPH'S CEMETERY, MOSTON, c. 1906

Opened in 1875, St. Joseph's Cemetery in Moston is the only cemetery in Manchester which is devoted entirely to Catholics. This particular view shows the Campo Santa which was completed in 1904. The cemetery itself has many memorials, but the most famous of them is that erected, in 1897, to three Fenians who were executed as a result of an attack on a police van on Hyde Road in September 1867, which resulted in the death of Sergeant Brett of the Manchester Police.

NEW MOSTON BOARD SCHOOL, MOSTON, c. 1905
With the passing of the Forster Education Act, School Boards were established in all districts to provide education for all children. The School Boards were separate from the local authorities and were given the task of building new schools or administering voluntary schools which had been handed to the board. Thie postcard shows the board school in New Moston, the design of which reflects many of the small, suburban board schools erected in the later 19th century.

BROOKDALE PARK, NEWTON HEATH, c. 1906

Brookdale Park lies on the edge of Newton Heath and like several other parks was the result of the acquisition by Manchester of a large private house and its grounds. Brookdale Park was originally owned by the Taylor family and was acquired by Manchester City Parks Department in 1900. The park, like others on the eastern side of the city, falls into two sections, divided by a stream and its valley. One park was laid out for sporting use whilst the remainder, centred on Brookdale Hall, was more formal with flower beds, walks, conservatory and lake.

ST. WILFRID'S CHURCH, NORTHENDEN

There has been a church in Northenden since before the Norman Conquest. It was built in a prominent position, overlooking the River Mersey and its ford, but above the flood plain. During the last 900 years, it has been restored and rebuilt on several occasions, the last time being in the 1870s. The architect for this major rebuilding of the church was J. S. Crowther, the architect to Manchester Cathedral, who copied the old style of the building although raising its height by 6 feet. The tower, however, was not rebuilt in the 1870s, but was subsequently restored in the 20th century.

ASHTON OLD ROAD, OPENSHAW

ASHTON OLD ROAD, OPENSHAW, 1919

Ashton Old Road was one of the original routes out of Manchester to the east. It passed through a number of settlements, one of which was Openshaw. In the 19th century, villages like Openshaw and its neighbour Gorton, attracted a lot of industry as they were outside the boundaries of Manchester and therefore had lower rates. They were, however, close enough to the city to attract skilled and other workers that were required. This photograph shows the junction of Ashton Old Road with Grey Mare Lane. In 1919, the buildings on the left included a bank, a greengrocer, an oyster dealer, a saddler, the Grey Mare Tavern, a telephone call office, a builder and a shirt manufacturer. On the opposite side of the road, the shops hid from view factories which included Armstrong Whitworth, the Metropolitan Carriage Works and Crossley's, all of which were adjacent to the railway from Manchester to Sheffield.

FAVOURITE WALK, GORTON RESERVOIR, HIGHER OPENSHAW.

GORTON RESERVOIRS, OPENSHAW, 1914

In the mid-1840s, Manchester realised that to improve the health of the town, there needed to be adequate supplies of clean water. As this could not be provided by the resources within the boundaries of Manchester, the council looked to the Longdendale valley in the Pennines. There was constructed a series of reservoirs. The water was then piped to storage reservoirs in Audenshawe and Gorton. The Gorton reservoirs were on the boundary of Gorton and Openshaw and provided an area which was not developed for housing and industry. The track along which the children are walking would have been constructed for vehicles requiring access to the reservoirs.

WILMSLOW ROAD, RUSHOLME, c. 1908

Wilmslow Road was originally part of the Manchester - Wilmslow Turnpike. By the mid-19th century, the area had reached the stage in its development where the existence of a turnpike road was not convenient and so maintenance of the section of Wilmslow Road through Rusholme became a public expense. This postcard shows the section of Wilmslow Road as it passes the former Manchester Carriage and Tramway Company's depot (on the left), which at its heyday housed over 700 horses. After the electrification of trams, the building became a riding school and then, in 1910, a cinema and finally the home of Rusholme Repertory Theatre.

79

WILMSLOW ROAD, RUSHOLME, 1910

Rusholme is divided into two sections by Wilmslow Road. This particular view of Wilmslow Road shows its junction with Platt Lane. Behind the trees on the left were Platt Cottage, Platt Abbey, Platt Terrace and Platt House, which date from the 19th century and were demolished in 1950 to be replaced by a block of flats. On the left can be seen the tower of Waterhouse's Rusholme Congregational Church which was opened in 1864. The church cost £7,000 and could seat 650 worshippers. It was demolished in 1978 after being unused for a number of years.

239J.   GRANGETHORPE HOSPITAL WILMSLOW ROAD. MANCHESTER   J L B SERIES

GRANGETHORPE HOSPITAL, RUSHOLME, 1929

This postcard of Grangethorpe Hospital was posted in 1929, the year when the building ceased to be a hospital and was sold, first to Manchester Royal Infirmary and then to Manchester High School for Girls, who demolished the building. The house itself was erected around 1882, almost certainly for a merchant family. The building exhibits features which were to be more widely adopted in the last decade of the 19th century, namely pseudo half-timbering and plaster work. This was a reaction to the Gothic style that had been in vogue earlier in the century and an attempt to revert back to something like the more traditional English domestic style of architecture. Despite this, there can still be seen some influence of the Gothic in the design.

PLATT FIELDS SPORTS PAVILION, RUSHOLME, 1921

Platt Fields was acquired by Manchester Corporation in 1907 after a private developer had purchased the site with the intention of demolishing the hall and building shops on the site. However, the purchaser was persuaded to sell the site to Manchester Corporation. The newly-created park was opened in June 1910 and included a large lake and a number of sports facilities, including a sports pavilion, pictured above.

HOLY TRINITY CHURCH, PLATT LANE, RUSHOLME, 1922

An important landmark from Platt Fields is the spire of Holy Trinity Church on Platt Lane. The church was built in 1846 and was one of the earliest churches to be built using terra cotta. It was designed by Edmund Sharpe and the cost, £5,600, was met by Thomas Carrill-Worsley of Platt Hall. The spire was rebuilt in 1910 as cracks were discovered in the terra cotta.

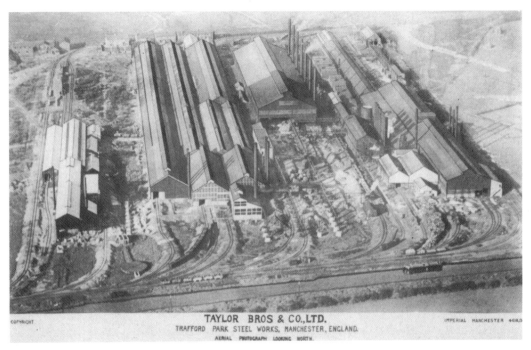

COPYRIGHT

TAYLOR BROS & CO.,LTD.
TRAFFORD PARK STEEL WORKS, MANCHESTER, ENGLAND.
AERIAL PHOTOGRAPH LOOKING NORTH.

IMPERIAL MANCHESTER 468.0

TAYLOR BROS., TRAFFORD PARK, c. 1910

Trafford Park was started in 1897 when the de Trafford family decided to sell their estates on the banks of the Manchester Ship Canal. Marshall Stevens had the idea of developing the area for industry, which could take advantage of the proximity of the Manchester Ship Canal for imports and exports. One firm which arrived there in 1907 was Taylor Brothers, who acquired a large site on the banks of the Bridgewater Canal for the manufacture of railway wheels and axles. The site was so large that Ashburton Road was deflected around it and did not go to Barton as originally intended.

BRITISH WESTINGHOUSE ELECTRIC AND MANUFACTURING CO., 1906

British Westinghouse Electric and Manufacturing Company was established in 1899 as an off-shoot of the Westinghouse Company of America. Work on erecting the building started in January 1901 and within 10 months, 8 of the 9 buildings were ready for use. This postcard shows the iron foundry which measured 578 feet by 170 feet. Amongst the early products the company made at Trafford Park was the equipment for the electrification of the Mersey Railway, gas engines and steam turbines for a variety of customers.

Entrance, Victoria Park, Longsight.

LONGSIGHT ENTRANCE, VICTORIA PARK, c. 1908

Victoria Park was planned in 1837, but the initial company formed to develop the area with large gentlemen's residences, suitable for Manchester's businessmen, was not a success. It was not until 1845 that a new organisation, the Victoria Park Trust, was established to look after and develop the area. In order to protect the residences from unwanted intrusion, there were gates at each of the entrances so that anyone wanting to pass through had to pay a toll. This postcard, sent as a Christmas card, shows the gate at the Longsight entrance to Victoria Park together with the gate-keeper's hut.

FIRST CHURCH OF CHRIST SCIENTIST, VICTORIA PARK, 1907
The First Church of Christ Scientist in Victoria Park was designed by the leading Manchester architect of the Arts and Crafts Movement, Edgar Wood, in 1903. Many of the architectural details of this fine building are typical of Wood and his work, which not only included public buildings, but also a number of houses in his home town of Middleton and in Hale; the latter being for Manchester businessmen and set amidst large gardens.

CRESCENT VICTORIA PARK MANCHESTER

THE CRESCENT, VICTORIA PARK, 1913

This postcard shows Hanover Crescent and the rural nature of Victoria Park when all around was built up with terraced houses. However, the exclusiveness of Victoria Park was already being eroded, with professional men building new houses and moving into an area which had been largely occupied by the merchant classes. A further encouragement to development had been given when the legal restrictions on building within the Park were abolished, and new semi-detached houses erected including ones on Daisy Bank Road, facing the road shown in the picture.

St. Joseph's Girls School, Victoria Park, Longsight.

ST. JOSEPH'S SCHOOLS, VICTORIA PARK, c. 1910

St. Joseph's Industrial Schools were established in Victoria Park to provide a Catholic education for the children of Catholics in the Victoria Park/Longsight area. The Catholic Church had had a presence in the area since 1865, when the Little Sisters of the Poor had moved from Higher Ardwick and established a convent in Victoria Park. The nuns, as well as providing assistance to the poor of the area, also used part of their convent for a girls' school. This postcard shows the building as it appeared in Edwardian times, before St. Joseph's Church was built on Plymouth Grove.

UPPER CHORLTON ROAD, WHALLEY RANGE, c. 1906

An important road out of Manchester on the south-western side of the city centre is Upper Chorlton Road. This view shows Upper Chorlton Road looking towards Brooks Bar. In the 19th century, much of the land in the area was owned by Samuel Brooks, who was not only involved in textiles, but also in banking. The church spire is that of Chorlton Road Congregational Church, built in 1860 to the designs of Poulton and Goodman. The houses on the right are typical of many of the houses built in the Whalley Range area in the late 19th century.

ALEXANDRA PARK. MAIN ENTRANCE

ALEXANDRA PARK, WHALLEY RANGE, 1906

The decision by Manchester to create a park in Moss Side raised legal problems as to whether a local authority could undertake work in another authority's area. It was decided that this was the case and in 1871, Alexandra Park was opened to the public. Amongst its many features were a lake, two gymnasia and a broad carriageway linking the two entrances. This postcard shows the Alexandra Road entrance with the lodge designed by Alfred Darbishire on the left and the gate piers designed by the City Surveyor in the centre.

ALEXANDRA PARK BANDSTAND, WHALLEY RANGE, 1905

An important feature of many 19th-century parks was the bandstand. This illustration shows the crowds listening to the band in Alexandra Park on a Sunday afternoon about 1905. The Parks Department regarded music in parks as very important and commented in 1915 that "A good performance of a band of music is not only an agreeable thing in itself, but makes an agreeable accompaniment to the enjoyment of a summer's evening or a Sunday afternoon in the parks. As at a garden party, it fits in with the pleasant surroundings, pervades the atmosphere with a spirit of melody and rhythm, and fills up the awkward breaks in conversation". Local brass bands were augmented by military bands in concerts which tended to be based on what may be described as the "light classics" such as works by Gilbert and Sullivan, Offenbach, Strauss, or the more popular works of the more serious composers like Verdi.

ST. BEDE'S COLLEGE, ALEXANDRA ROAD, WHALLEY RANGE, 1906

St. Bede's College was built in 1872 by the Manchester Aquarium Company Limited as there was an upsurge of interest in aquaria not only in other parts of the country, but also in Europe. The project was not a success and in 1878, it was closed and the building sold to the Catholic Church to provide a home for the rapidly expanding St. Bede's College. Part of the building continued to be used as a museum until 1886, when it was converted into a hall and chapel. The Italianate building presents a striking backdrop to Alexandra Park, which it faces across Alexandra Road.

WITHINGTON RD.

Best wishes for Xmas & love from L. Barrow.

WITHINGTON ROAD, WHALLEY RANGE, 1904

Withington Road has two distinct sections: smaller houses north of Yarbugh Street and large, detached houses occupied by business and professional men to the south of the road. This postcard, sent to someone living in Chile, shows some of the mid-Victorian houses on the southern section of Withington Road. Many of the houses had names such as "Beechfield", "Ennerdale House", "Wittenburg" and "Suffolk House". They were occupied by merchants and business men such as James Swales, a brewer, H. J. Cutter, chief clerk at the High Court and S. H. Owen, surgeon. Another important building on Withington Road was Whalley Range High School for Girls, which is still in existence today.

HARDEY'S VICTORIA COLLEGE, ALEXANDRA ROAD SOUTH, WHALLEY RANGE, c. 1914
When this Methodist training college was established in 1879, this part of Whalley Range was still relatively rural in its appearance. The portion of the building on the left was built in 1879 whilst the clock tower was erected in 1896. Further building took place in the early 20th century when the rest of the complex was completed, including the chapel.

21815   WITHINGTON.

WILMSLOW ROAD, WITHINGTON, c. 1910

During the latter half of the 19th century, Withington was first a local board of health, and then an urban district council that covered not only modern Withington, but also Didsbury and Chorlton-cum-Hardy. The main road through Withington is Wilmslow Road, along whose length are to be found most of the shops that served this area. On the left, can be seen the Withington branch of the Manchester and County Bank and, next door to it, Withington Methodist Church, which opened in 1865 and cost £3000. The shop between the bank and the chapel was occupied in 1911 by George Leather, draper. The block of shops on the opposite side of the road included Hewitt's, a well-known newsagent in the area, a butcher's shop and a china dealer's premises.

WITHINGTON PARISH CHURCH, c. 1902

St. Paul's Church, Withington, consecrated in 1841, was built to serve the growing communities of Withington, Ladybarn, Fallowfield and Burnage. It was designed by Hayley and Brown in the Gothic style at a cost of £3,849, including furnishings and fittings. The site was given by William Egerton who also contributed £400 towards the cost of building the church. As with many churches built at the time, St. Paul's had only 277 free seats, pew rents being charged for the remainder of the 649 seats. At the end of the century, the church had 750 seats of which 504 were free. Today all are free.

WITHINGTON GREEN.

WITHINGTON GREEN, WITHINGTON

Withington Green may be the remains of the old village green in Withington. It is bounded on the Northern side by Cotton Lane, with is not connected with cotton, but probably with the fact that land in the area was shared by three adjoining townships, each township using the land for a year. The Tithe map indicates that the Green was in private ownership at the time the survey was undertaken and that it was used as meadow by John Thornley, who appears to have farmed about 54 acres in and around the Green. By the time this postcard was issued, the farms had disappeared and large houses, set in their own grounds, surrounded it.

PALATINE ROAD, WITHINGTON, 1904

Palatine Road came into existence as a result of an agreement between the Manchester and Wilmslow Turnpike Trust and Withington Local Board of Health, that the latter would not object to the renewal of the Trusts Act of Parliament if a new road and crossing of the River Mersey was constructed. The result was Palatine Road, which soon was lined with the large residences of Manchester's businessmen like the ones which can be seen behind the trees on this postcard.

WITHINGTON STATION, WITHINGTON, c. 1905

Withington Station opened in 1880 when the Midland Railway completed their line from New Mills via Stockport Tiviot Dale into Manchester Central Station. The opening of the station, which was located where Withington and West Didsbury met, brought their area within 10 minutes travelling time of central Manchester, with trains up to 1 a.m. both to and from Manchester. Even before the railway had been completed, the land close to the station had been laid out for housing, most of which was semi-detached and intended for professional men and their families.

COPYRIGHT NELL LANE HOSPITAL, MANCHESTER. N.S.R. ROCHDALE

WITHINGTON HOSPITAL, 1945

Withington Hospital was originally Chorlton Union Workhouse. The first buildings on the site were erected in 1856 and the hospital blocks (centre back) were designed by Thomas Worthington and added in 1865. Worthington was an architect with a social conscience and consulted Florence Nightingale over the design of the wards and hence they were of the highest standards. For example: all the sanitation was kept to one end of the building so that access to the sewers was simplified compared with other large institutional buildings. The workhouse could house over 1000 inmates, many of whom by the end of the 19th century were elderly, infirm or suffering from mental disorders. When the poor law was replaced by modern social welfare provisions, Withington Workhouse was transformed into a hospital serving south Manchester.

WYTHENSHAWE PARK

Wythenshawe Park surrounds Wythenshawe Hall, a black and white building dating from the 16th century. Until 1926, it was owned by the Tatton family, who sold it to the Simons who in turn passed it to Manchester. This postcard has the manuscript note on the back that it is Wythenshawe Park, and although at first it seems incongruous that a private estate should have refreshment rooms, the park itself was a popular venue for Sunday School outings and possibly other groups, hence the need to provide some form of refreshment facilities for visitors.

CROSSACRES, GATLEY.

CROSSACRES, WYTHENSHAWE, c. 1918

When this postcard was sent about 1918, Crossacres was part of Cheadle and Gatley and did not become part of Manchester until 1931. The view shows one of the three farms in the area. These were farmed by Samuel Johnson, William Shenton at Peel Hall and John Johnson. As the buildings do not appear to be surrounded by a moat, as Peel Hall was, it is probable that the farm was occupied either by Samuel or John Johnson. The road was given an official name in 1930, but it is not clear whether this one is Peel Hall Road or Crossacres Road.

Sharston Manor and Mount Gatley.

ALTRINCHAM ROAD, SHARSTON, WYTHENSHAWE, c. 1910
Today this quiet country lane is a busy main road linking Cheadle with Altrincham. It is, in fact, Altrincham Road, around the beginning of the 20th century. The two houses referred to on the title of the card were both large 18th-century houses which would have served as farm-houses; agriculture being an important employer of labour in the area until the 1930s.

104

SHARSTON. GATLEY

SHARSTON, 1918

One of the more important buildings in Sharston, which like Crossacres was part of Cheadle and Gatley until 1931, was Sharston Hall, which is partially hidden behind the trees on the left of the picture. The hall is said to date from 1701 although the earliest reference to it is from 1754. The core of the building was Georgian, but there were many alterations made to it in the 19th century. The Worthington family were the original occupiers of the hall, but at the time the photograph was taken, the occupier was Robert Clay.

TEA ROOMS, SHARSTON

Sharston was a popular place for visitors from the surrounding towns in the late 19th and early 20th centuries. To serve the needs of the visitors, the tea rooms depicted on this postcard were opened in 1901 in a converted schoolroom. The building itself dates from 1869 when the old school had become insanitary and served not only Sharston, but also Northenden, pupils having to walk along unlit and unmade roads to school. As well as being a tea room, the building was also used for religious services; there being a shortage of accommodation for this purpose in the area.

SHARSTON, WYTHENSHAWE, 1912

This postcard shows the teachers of Stockport Sunday School on 31st August, 1912 on a trip into the country. The venue of their visit that year appears to have been Sharston. It would have been relatively easy for them to have reached the area as there were electric trams running from Stockport into Gatley and it would have been only a short walk along quiet roads into Sharston.

CHAMBER HALL, WYTHENSHAWE, c. 1906

Chamber Hall stands close to the border between Manchester, Cheadle and Gatley, and was part of that authority until Wythenshawe became part of Manchester. The hall was built around 1703 and may occupy the site of an earlier building. The building was occupied by the Shelmerdine family for several generations, there being the letters "M S M" on a rainwater spout. There is no explanation as to why this building was called Chamber Hall, but it may be because it was the first house in the area to have separate chambers or bedrooms upstairs.

DONKEY CARRIAGE, c. 1906

This postcard shows an interesting form of personal transport in one of Manchester's suburbs. The message on the back refers to "Mother and her Menagerie" and is signed the "Menagerie Monkey". Presumably this was a personal photograph that was turned into a postcard for the use of the family. The menagerie probably refers to the donkey and the animal being held by the person standing on the pavement.

LAST POST SERVICE, c. 1918

It has not been possible to discover what the "Last post service" was or when it was held or whether it was peculiar to a particular church or denomination. It is possible that it was an event held in connection with remembering those people from the church who had died during the First World War. As with some other postcards in this book, it appears that this was a private photograph turned into a postcard as there is a note on the back which reads: "They are not very good, they are too dark" indicating that it had been taken by an amateur photographer.

ALEXANDRA PARK, MANCHESTER.

D.F & C York.

NIGHT TIME AT ALEXANDRA PARK

Sometimes interesting postcards are published which do not show buildings or events or people, but rather a particular time of day. This one shows night over Alexandra Park with the lights of St. Bede's College in the background. The message on the back is very apt for this scene - it reads: "Meet me by moonlight alone Dear". One wonders whether the meeting actually took place and if so, did the couple have a "heavenly time"!

Having a Heavenly Time at Manchester

"HAVING A HEAVENLY TIME AT MANCHESTER"

This is not what many people would have thought about Manchester in the early years of the 20th century, but no doubt it was an attempt by the postcard manufacturers to add a little bit of light relief to the range of cards published on Manchester. The view is of the Manchester Ship Canal, looking towards Manchester from Mode Wheel. Clearly visible on the right are the extensive timber wharfs and Trafford Park. Perhaps is might be a follow-up to the previous postcard's message!

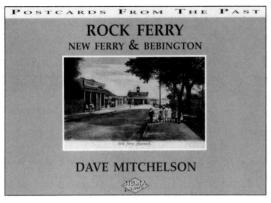

POSTCARDS FROM THE PAST: ROCK FERRY, NEW FERRY & BEBINGTON

Dave Mitchelson

This is the companion book to "Old Bebington" (also published by Sigma Leisure) and is based on the author's extensive collection. Memories will flood back for local people as they see how Rock Ferry was once a leafy village with fine old buildings and fascinating local personalities.

£6.95

POSTCARDS FROM THE PAST: WREXHAM

Gwyneth Williams

Take a lingering look into Wrexham's past with this excellent selection of black and white postcards. The collection gives an insight into the way that the town has developed over the years, whilst evoking nostalgic memories of the old ways of life. Will fascinate residents and those interested in local history.

£6.95

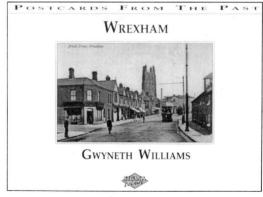

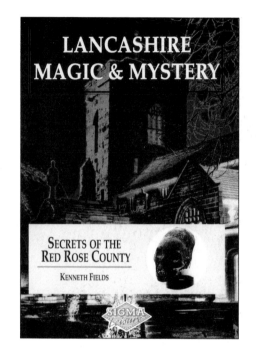

LANCASHIRE MAGIC & MYSTERY: Secrets of the Red Rose County

Kenneth Fields

Covering all of Lancashire, including Merseyside and Greater Manchester, Ken Field's new book will guide you to places of mystery and curiosity. With tales of hauntings, witchcraft, religious relics, folklore and UFOs, this book is a must for anyone interested in local mythology and folk lore. It will appeal to both visitors and residents, and also the increasing number of armchair travellers who relish the secret history of the landscape. The author enjoys exploring all aspects of the English countryside and contributes regularly to magazines. This is his fourth book for Sigma.

£6.95

You can order our books from any bookseller. In case of difficulty, or for a free catalogue, please contact:
SIGMA LEISURE, 1 SOUTH OAK LANE, WILMSLOW, CHESHIRE SK9 6AR. Phone: 01625-531035; Fax: 01625-536800.
E-mail: sigma.press@zetnet.co.uk . Web site: http//www.sigmapress.co.uk
Credit card orders welcome. Please add £2 p&p to all orders.